UH-FLIK-SHUHN

D1570430

By
Alphonso Nkruma Flowers

DEDICATION

This book is dedicated to those in the struggle but have not lost hope. To those who choose to stare every giant in the face, through faith, overcoming their ominous front, then laying hold to the vision and dreams set before them. This book is dedicated to those who understand that a moment of **Uh-Flik-Shuhn** cannot be compared to the glory that shall be revealed!

Acknowledgements

Any project, performance, expression of art, or business is brought to life with grit, faith, vision, and love. Therefore, I would like to acknowledge Fiverr for creating a platform in which talented and skilled professionals are able to show-case their own God given gifts and talents in efforts of helping manifest the visions and dreams of others. Thank you, GermanCreative Les for taking my elementary concept of a book cover and bringing it to absolute LIFE! Thank you, Oprah of OprahGraphic, for taking my attempt of structuring this book and giving BREATH to its pages, presentable for all to enjoy. Thank you, to my good friend and work buddy Alicia Stansbury for taking the time to "edit after editing" (you should know the book by heart). And to those that have taken the time to read and give an honest critique of my work. Love Yawl to the fullest. Lastly, thank each and every reader, supporter, encourager, and artistic expression that has inspired me to step out the norm and into a stream of life that has been dying to live.

The Song Writer, Alphonso Nkruma Flowers.

Uh-Flik-shuhn

Foreword

Uh-Flik-shuhn- So many ails plague society. Seems, daily we fail to reach standards set by our ancestors while falling into insatiable lusts and dark regions of heart and mind. Lovers of men, more than lovers of God!

Our eyes have become dim and our ears dull of hearing, failing to acknowledge the clarion call, killing ourselves in ignorance. We have sat in the lukewarm waters of life far too long, unable to discern the intense fire that now threatens our lives. Slowly boiling, slowly dying!

Uh-Flik-shuhn- has way of making us or breaking us, turning us back to God or pushing us away; if we fail to heed the lesson given, our lives may slip silently away- into the night!

Many times *Uh-Flik-shuhn* is the chastening hand of our faithful, merciful, and longsuffering creator- desiring we return, come home!
Psalms 34:19

Affliction!

Rebuild The Walls

Before there was sin, I was free
Before coats of skin, there was me
Before I was blind, I could see
Before there was God
Now idolatry

Rebuild The Walls

Awakenings

Dark skies
No stars that shine
The moon it hides
Behind the earth
Chill of night
Sighs of fright
Pain before
Earth gives birth
To sunny days
Joyous times
Birds that sing
Butterflies
Smiles to cries
Vines to dearth
Death to life
Anguish to birth

Awakenings

Humanity!

One can only hide so long
We shake hands facetiously
Ear to ear, a smile upon face
What lies in that secret place?
Where eyes cannot see, ears cannot hear
Where words proceed, oh so clear
Where dark visions may oft appear
That house our loved ones held so dear

Those fighting words are hard to retract?
The hatred because my skin is black
The racial slurs, the verbal attacks
The sinister chuckles, the envious laughs
Are you disturbed because I'm white?
Boils your blood to the point of fights
Makes you cut such hateful eyes
So hardened that tears never fall from your eyes
You chuckle and sneer at my skin so brown?
Judge my language with different sound
Makes you want to always throw down
Until the blood falls to the ground

Why do you hate the color of me?
Distorted views you have of me?
Am I that different for fear of me
We cannot join hands and be free

Humanity

The Day I Died!

The Day I Died-
Was the day I ceased from my own regard
Was the day fear no longer governed my life
Was the day I crucified my passions
Was the day I loved without strife

The Day I died-
Was the day I gave without acclaim
Was the day my enemies remembered my name
Was the day the face of humanity looked the same
Was the day God's Spirit led the way

The Day I Died-
Was the day I ceased from my own understanding;
Standing in Fear of God

The Day I lived!

Poetic Whispers

Will the poet ever grasp
Whispers spoken in soul
Reflective of humanities cry
Nature's movement or God's wisdom
Flirting with the flame of love
Daunting as one tries to convey
Mysteries
Dark revelations
Truths
Speaking more volumes than the seas
Captured in thoughts
Notions
Unction's
From the Eternal Father
Bringing awareness into the hearts of men
How bitter-sweet
How heavy yet light
How dark yet illuminating
This soul handed down from our Creator
That we may be the expression
Of His Glory on the earth-
That we may render unyielding love
It is a wonder
Too deep to grasp
Invested into the pith of our being
The pulse nurturing our very soul-
Heart to heart, breast to breast
If the tongue speaks to life
It stems from fruit within
To live suggests, you feast of its fruit
Perplexing, how winds of adversity
Has way of resurrecting the voice of victory
Victory which stands bold; relentless
With new mercies granted

We embark upon each day
As a baby birthed from the womb
What lies ahead?
What blessing waits?
What miracle to be revealed?
Searching
Anticipating
Expecting
Blessings to come
However, life may be cold
Unmerciful
Seemingly, prejudice as to whom it favors
I find, as the chilled breeze of morning
Blows across my face
Life, nature, the universe
Also goes through changes-
Birthed from earth's womb
Not only our spiritual
But natural soul
Can feel the nervousness
The turning
The pangs
Of our universe's
Parturition
Stresses the cosmos
If not grounded, chaos and utter darkness
All to preserve you and I
As whispers come and go
Emotions to and fro
To capture the essence of one whisper told
Can change life forever
Enlightening eyes
Or, leaving blind what is already closed
Eyes which fail to see the light

Poetic Whispers-

Soul & Spirit

So precious
Delicate
Expressive
Untouchable
Yet touching many.
Invisible, though more color
More color than rainbows, botanical gardens
A coral reef, floral arrangement, or the Blues
Searching as a lost child
Finding its way,
Searching as love
Seeks a place for its head to lie,
Inviting, as the lushes lips
Or unending curves of a woman's anatomy;
Hiding unseen treasure
Such profound mystery, exquisite!
More powerful than oceans, forces of nature
Enduring the fire that tries
The breath of time, everlasting
The life in smiles
Rhythm in blood
Tenderness in touch
Butterflies of attraction
The quiver in making love
The dexterity of thought
Visions to dreams
Cleansing in tears
Faith in the unseen
The willingness to be
The strength of letting go
Precious
Inquisitive
Progressing
I n f I n I t e

No More Faces

What do you do when no more faces,
As they wane in the midst of night
What do you do when no more places,
Your mind can take flight

What do you do when no more songs,
Of love your heart can sing
What do you do when eyes are empty,
Full of shallow dreams

What do you do when no more reason,
To hope for love at all
What do you do when no more hand,
To pick you up when you fall

What do you do when your inspiration,
Has drifted with the wind
What do you do when your ink runs dry,
No more poetry to your pen

What do you do when no more kisses,
To appease your longing soul
What do you do when words won't form,
To express an inner void

Love it seems to come and go
But was it really there
Or insatiable lust arresting the soul
To think that someone cared

Maybe a fire set a blazed
That could not be contained
Maybe the pillow that holds your head
In times of silent pain

What do you do?
How do you smile?
With images in your mind
No one to touch
No one to love
No one to pass the time

No More Faces

Raging Waters

How can one verbalize
A movement unprecedented
Raging in the soul
Wind gushing to and fro
A sound of thunderous proportions
I heard it before
The sound of raging waters
During a time
When the flickering light of the candle
Was put to rest
When life seemed, silent moments in time
Deafening!
The howl
Clouds tumbling one after the other
Dark comforting stillness
Sitting at a table
Under depressed light
Under intense pressure
How can one define
Moments of shadowing clarity-
As if contrary winds
Brushing across the face,
Moving through the hair,
Pressing upon each and every member
Of fragile clay
Rushing through the eardrum,
Piercing the soul
I hear the Voice speak
"There shall be Life"
Life will endure
Life will live- birthing
Though outstanding opposition

The cool and terrific wind that blows
The sounds of rushing waters
The sounds of eternal storms
Blowing though the firmament
Enduring life
Turning the soul as a whirlwind
Setting motion what is to come

Raging Waters

Mighty Congo

Mighty Congo run swift and wild
So terrible
Invigorating
Breath taking
The sound of your voice brings chills to my spine-
Deep bellows,
Crashing wave upon wave,
You stir my soul with depths unsearchable to human eye.
Current upon current
Level upon level
Your mysterious flux-
Rapids, streams, lively hood,
Ecosystem leaves me in state of bewilderment
Such creatures of awesome sight-
Such creatures of Awesome God!
River so raging you perpetuate life
Depths so deep giving birth to unseen mystery-
Unseen glory!
Forcing such to take on new name
New character
New strength
In efforts to endure your awesome terror!
The wisdom of unnatural behavior
Both concealed and revealed through your bosom.
When separated by opposing streams
Nature must evolve-
Lest nature dies.
Such monstrosities become gods
Or taboo,
Or legends

Justifying nature's aggression to survive-
Like the Congo Wild
Souls are beguiled
By unnatural currents in life, unnatural behavior,
Separated by its vicious flow-
Leave us searching for that missing link,
Yes, searching for the other part of me.
Mighty Congo run swift and free
May we learn the depths of your glory!
May we give reverence to your story!
Lest we, carried away by such dark wonder
Fail to embrace simplicity of life!

REST

Last night I held you
In no defined terms
We sat close to each other's side
Love was there, but not in our eyes

The tenderness, the comfort
The assurance of not being alone
Our bodies wrapped in solace
The solitaire made strong

Though different in gender
Though different space and time
The cry of your heart
Was felt in mine

Two souls in flight
We met in night
Transcending flesh
To share a breath

Of

Friendship
Compassion
Sincerity
Strength

Quaint
As you lay your head upon my chest

Rest

Forgetting woes which trouble your soul
In yearning to be heard
Yet blinded eyes cannot behold

Rest

Cast away the burdens
You uphold day by day
Cast them upon God who cares
Who will bottle your tears away

Rest

For your tears will turn to joy
And love will replenish
For it flows like a river
From the corridors of Heaven

Rest

Know in confidence
That you are not alone
For visions of night
May give life to plight
As you are made strong

Rest

I Rest

As I read the writing on the wall
Holding my chest as if my heart
For fear that, it will fail
Hearing silent cries while children wail
So much misdirection
So many dreams suffocated
By sensuous lure of the streets; empty promises of stardom
Icons are dying away
Seems the world is headed that way
As if their inspiration has been, taken away
Drifting on a memory

I Rest

Praying the light will shine
Praying the end of crime
Praying our children will find
Peace and direction for their minds
Praying our fathers come home
Praying daughters no longer roam
Praying our mothers stay strong
Praying our brothers love deeper
That they may become my brother's keeper

I Rest

In the unfailing mercy of God.

One Can't Help But Cry!

Viewing the face of humanity, my heart saddens-
The disconnect cuts deep
This cesspool of ego and selfishness burns with deadening stench-
Woe in community!
One can't help cry tears of stone
So many hearts have grown cold.
What can we do but lay at our Creators feet
'Til forgiveness, healing, flow from His throne!
We are in need of his guidance.

If Eternity lay in the palm of His Hand,
What is my end?
Life can be so viscous,
Life can tear you limb from limb,
Then gone to yonder place.
No prejudice, no racism,
Now inward hate, no envy,
Just life in its season, no reason.
How can I dictate my own fate
When I don't have power over death, or power to give life?
Every man must die- what if before time?
Will he live again?

We live as if god's holding the future in our hand
Conquering our fellow man, for what?
We're all men.
If I can hear cries from the spilt blood of my brothers
Why are you trying to kill me?
We all bleed!
We are all part of the same, all God's creation-
God's beautiful creation!
What gives anyone the right to take such precious life?
Whether by oppression, manipulation,
Thievery, trickery,

When I look in the mirror,
I see you,
But do you see me?

I hear blood from the heart of God, rushing like rivers
Deep into the heart of Earth
To the edge of night- gushing
Because we've bruised him again
Even after giving his life in efforts to reconcile with man!
We deny the Truth
We deny we've abused
We shut our cores of compassion
Leaving our own blood out like prey
Skillfully Hunted

One Can't Help But Cry

Time is but a wind
Our lives but a vapor
Our hearts but a fading tune
Our minds but a ticking clock
Ticking closer to expiration
Will we capture the moment and
Every chance we have to love
That we may express such tenderness
Lest we allow it to slip away missing life
Yes, missing a chance to live again- Eternal

One Can't Help But Cry!

Can You Hear The Cries?

Do you remember the times
Leaving your front door unlocked
Was no problem at all?
Off to work
Off to school
Then back home, and
Everything was cool
Days when neighbors would literally put a strap
To your hide
If they caught you acting up
Or getting beat up in fights
When it was safe to roam the streets
Man, you could not beat
The simple liberties that no longer exist today
When did we lose site of the way?
Who planted the tares
As we slept the night away?
Who unlock the door
And gave thieves the right-away
To destroy the structure of family
Violate the sanctify of marriage
Seems as if we've all miscarried
Generations of tomorrow
I think we need to borrow
A lesson from the eagle
Devoted to love
Devoted to raising up its sons
Until matured enough to handle
The depth of their vision
But today we give them
Reward without pain
Children without name
Blessings with no test
Life with no breath

What's left
But rebellion in the name of liberty?
What about you, it's all about me
My house
My car
My bling
Fake breast
Fake nails
Fake weave
Fake realities & goals we'll never achieve
I can't believe
Yesterday I was waking to brighter skies
Today I wake & hear the cries
Of babies killing babies & no one sighs
Just movement
Busy doing nothing
Talking loud, and saying nothing
Eyes full of lust and always wanting
More to consume
Eyes half-mast & doom
One-step away
One breath away
One yes away
Knowledge is key
But we've unlocked the evil
Exploited its presence
Having succumbed to its essence
Dance to its music
Bodies we've abused it
The light we've refused
And call it amusement
We've spent the last few decades
Cooling in the shade
As though we've got it made
But yet we've missed the grade
Of discipleship
Now our youth are being pimped
Thinking that's the latest hip- whipped

One can't help but be saddened
Who passed the baton?
Who was supposed to grab it?
When did it slip from our finger-tips
Into the hands of crude politics
Jesus said
Forsake not the children to come
For such is the kingdom of heaven
But now, full of leaven
Because we've failed to give them 7
7 years of tender love
7 more years of kisses and hugs
7 more years of sincere tuff love
Before they embark upon
7 more years, of pursuing dreams from the Creator above
Pardon me
There is more to life than just me
But reaching & teaching that the world may see
God above
Is yet waiting to share his love
Through faith in his Only Begotten Son
The One who died
The Life and the Light that shines
In the heart of men, resides
Birthing us into new life
Until it's time to be lifted above the skies
Tell me

Can you hear the cries?

Of babies momma's
No longer strong enough to handle the drama
Father's love has rolled away
Babies left on steps one day
Into the system the next
We wonder why the earth is vexed
Yearning for the sons of God to stand
That they may usher in
The Glorious return of the Son of man
Now making intercession for fallen man
Are we doing the best we can?
Or are we dancing to our own colorful band,
Our own music?
Will we join and start a movement?
A movement of peace & love,
It's never too late
Until fate knocks on the door,
And we no longer wake
The day that death takes our life away
When our souls are carried to life away
Let's stay upon our knees
Until we reach the heavenly places
Where God graces
Bringing him down
Down to the gutter
Down to our sisters & brothers
Down to the unknown & others
Down to single mothers & fathers
Down to the family system
Down to political systems
Down to our churches & homes
Down to our very soul
Let's forgive the lies and break the ties
Constantly causing tears to fall from our eyes!

Can You Hear The Cries?

Dying In The Night

I

Children no longer bear the iniquity of their fathers
Every man must bear his own
Where does responsibility lie?
How heavy the tears which fall from our eyes
Do we have hands strong enough to hold together the ties- of
Family?
Are we independently running
Gunning after our own future
Engrossed with our own vision
That we fail to live in, community?
Causing divide that we may prod around in senseless pride
As if, the world revolves around I.

       God never intended for man to live alone
       God wanted love to fill their home
       God wanted family to represent his own
       God never intended for his children to roam

The effects of heeded instruction are grave.
Eternity rests beyond the grave.
Who will lead us through the narrow way
When so many choose the wider way?
Our duty lies before us
God's Word doth soundly implore us
To live as lights though darkness before us
Let Love be the band which holds us
Molds us
Shapes us
Breaks us
In efforts to make us
Fathers and mothers
Sons and daughters
Of God

II

Are the watchmen watching?
Are Prophets of God talking?
Are the Faith-full walking?
Are hedges being resurrected
That our families be protected,
From thieves seeking to kill, steal, and destroy?
I can hear the hearts of sons
Crying out for truth looking for someone
Who won't judge to quick
But stick around until change comes.
Change will come!
For better or for worse!
But who?
Who will dirty their knees?
Who will stand in the gap?
Declaring our sons shall live
Change must come but we must hear it in the ear!
We must hear it in faith
We must hear it from sleep to wake
We must take our fate by the mane
Stare it in the face and declare victory!
Tell me
Are we laying our lives down that our sons may be found?
Ushered into destiny,
Led to their seats of royalty,
Taught how to speak,
Bold when they reach,
Full of knowledge when they teach?

We have paid for homes and education
Yet, there lies a vacant space, communication!
Heart to heart we must bridge the gap,
We must be the first to act,
Lest they be swallowed up in the streets.
The feat is great, but it is not too late
As breath fills the lungs,
As life gives birth,
We can make the change
While living,
But we must give in- to our own

III

The smell of blood fills the air
The sound of tears falling everywhere
The voice of rebellion causing a scare
Steps of men and women running in fear
Have we turned a death ear?
Dead to the cry of mercy
Dead to the cry of humanity
Dead to the voice of love
Dead to the voice of God
We have crossed so many lines
So much confusion the whole head is sick
The winds of adversity are causing a shift
Shaking the right from the wrong
The weak from the strong
The clean from those that don't belong
What's going on?
We have hardened our hearts to the voice of God
The answer rings crystal clear but do we hear?
Yet we wonder why our sons don't hear us
Nor do they fear us!
My heart cries out that God will save us
Then shape us to be who he has called us to be
Created in His image and likeness
It will take fathers and mothers
Crying out to God as our sons and daughters cry out to us.
Having ears to hear instruction
Leading to Eternity's Rest
On the other side of heaven, we know
The time is critical
We have hung so many out to dry
Then gloat about being upright
Yet our sons and daughters are

Dying In The Night!

We've Left Them To Roam!

We've left them to roam
Here to there no place to call home
No face to call mom or dad
Sister or brother
From this path to that path
In search of identity
Have we aborted a generation?
In search for identity
Have we aborted a generation?
They say X marks the spot but what did you see
Was it human nature and its selfish motives blinded by darker light?
Was it a baby dropped in flight?
Like Mephibosheth, by the one who should have carried him to safety?
The family
The home
The church
The friends
The loved ones
Now crippled
Unable to stand on his own
Plan on his own
Be a man on his own
Who would dare
To sit him in his rightful place
A king or disgraced

We've Left Them To Roam

Like bicycles from this place to that place
Spinning round and round
Feet never touching the ground- spinning
Seemingly never a sound moment
To take it all in
Coming going like the wind

Drifting
In and out of everything that tickles the fancy
No stability
No direction
Yet following erections to satisfy affections
And open invitations
To those wanting soothing for the burning of their yearning
Aggravations
Our cities are burning!
Infested with sickness and dis-ease
Incurable H I V., Aids
To unstoppable hearts which bleed
Such dark loneliness
Willing to be up our blessed-ness
To be intimate unaffectionate
Spinning out of control
No brakes
No one to hold
Like bicycles from this place to that place

We've Left Them To Roam

When freedom sounded
Did we stay grounded to the fight
Of how to live free while keeping our families tight
Struggle has a way of birthing us
Sometimes I feel freedom's hurting us
Now I feel God is urging us
To get our house in order, the end's approaching us
Time for the hearts of fathers to turn back to their sons
Back to the days when they played and laughed in the Son
When they played hide and seek but look what we've become
Don't ask me for help I don't have the time
You didn't work for this- this money is mine
True, a hard head will make a soft behind
However, a provoked and hardened heart may never heal in time
May lead to crime
May lead to women of the night selling their soul for a dime

May lead to reprobate minds
May lead to souls going to hell because we don't have time
For the community of family
Let's break this insanity
Let's run after our sons
You know the ones
Who don't belong to you
Or, maybe they do

We've Left Them To Roam

There's a dearth in the streets
The sound of family
The sound of mommy and daddy
The sound of joy, unity and glee
The sound of being free
Have we blamed it on our sons?
Birthing babies, now full grown, yet afraid to give hugs
Due to the fact, emptiness resides where there should have been Love
Have we blamed it on our daughters?
Birthing babies then loving them more than their fathers
Expressing what they've learned from selfish mothers and fathers
Now full-grown and don't want to be bothered
So much to fix
So little time
It takes God to heal a generation
Being put to the grind
A void, in search of finding its mind
Before they're erased- from pages of time

We've Left Them To Roam

Winter To Spring

I.

Spring hangs in the balance
Winter not willing to let go
Dreams uneasy warring within
Sensing new life beginning

Between seasons,
We oft loose site of our passion
Open to adversaries taunting
Drawing us from purpose
Faith somehow seems to wane
Beneath the gentle breeze as chilling snow

Stagnate between winters charm, and
Springs enticing kiss of joy
We perplexed with vast emotion
Have tendency to drift in the wind
Hoping purpose will manifest to fulfillment

Transitions can seem breath taking
Change at times can shake our very foundation
Growth may bring with it great pain
Shifting may cause us to lose focus

How do we quantify arriving in our season?
While enduring the affliction appointed for our lives
The reasons of a dawning sun
Seems as a mist from winter's rain
A bountiful blanket of life upon the horizon
Yet out of touch just out of reach
Will Spring come again~ here I stand?

33

Navigating through such transition, blessedness
Presents with it a new feat each day
A new dilemma
A new opportunity to learn
A new opportunity to love
A new opportunity to live
A new opportunity to die
Like the butterfly from its cocoon, captivating to the eye
Destined to the prudent; teaching the maturation process of life.

How do we so effortlessly fall into vice
When we have fought vigorously to break free?
Are we simply struggling to break through to the divine?
Transforming into immortality?
Are we bound to such habitation of flesh
As our spirits cry out to live?
Are we destined to a grave which keeps its secrets
Revealed to those who enter its realm of unknown rest?
Are we traveling in a strange land as pilgrims searching for a place to call home?

As seasons come and go
We are transformed
We are captives of time and change
We are compelled to embrace its lesson
Understand its folly
Rejoice in its victory
Take comfort in its care
Love during its need
To keep moving with its current.

As winter breaks
The need to understand life ahead
Stirs the passion desiring to go free
Kissing the lips of Spring
Expecting all that it will bring!

II.

We live today as if forever
Chasing the wind as it blows
We build upon dreams
But do we ever
Consider where OUR spirits will go?

Truth doth call
While in pursuit we run
Searching the mysteries of life
Our souls do reach
For heavens beseech
Calling us to Her abode

Such enflamed desire,
Such longing persists,
Within the city of OUR soul
Yet prodigals run
In lust for fun
Not mindful of where they may roam.

From hog pens of life
We lift our eyes
Never satisfied of OUR hearts desire
Though good the intent
We'll never be content
Driven by such fleshly fire

Consuming,
Destroying,
All in its path;
Burning profusely, enraged
Such imperfections in man
How do we dare stand?
Without the help of Heaven's hand?

CAPTIVE

I.

I hear Love calling
Its pleasant voice caressing my skin
Like a gentle rain
Opening my pours to its cleansing
To its life-giving touch

I smile for I welcome Love's company

It's in such times
I entreat Love to embellish me
With its intrigue and wisdom
Speaking to the invisible soul
I embrace all given;
Passionately musing upon words said
That I may appropriate its lesson
To such desperate life

To be in the presence of Love
Is to step into Eternity
Is to forget present woes
Is to escape fleshly vices
Is to commune with soul and spirit
Is intimacy with the Almighty!
It's in such times
The desire to leave this earthen vessel
Becomes so pressing, that
To dwell at the foot of Love
I'd crucify the very craving of my heart to live.
Dying to live
Living to die
That I may be
With Love

II.

The affliction
The perplexing
The turmoil arises
When Love must continue its journey
Many are in need of its sustaining touch
Many await its arrival, selfishly
Desiring to keep Love, to themselves.
Yet, realizing the need of this dark world
Fighting for
Praying for crying for
Its touch, and
Such words, which fall as drops of honey;
Filling the panting soul.

I'm panting!

One would think
After entertaining Love, embracing its lesson
Life would unfold like a rose;
Praising the sun while basking in its glory.
Yet the suffering reality is how to express,
How to satisfy,
How to articulate,
Our souls thirsting for such affection

III.

Roses are Red
Violets are Blue
Was it a blessing or curse
The day I found you
Love is
Life giving, breath taking
Sweet to the soul, rotten to the bone
Electrifying, horrifying
Full of joy and intense crying

As we search for love
In the smile of others
We foolishly embark on the impossible
Love, taught from Love itself
We are to express what's handed down
As legacy to posterity;
Kings to royalty

The blessing, Love is eternal
The curse we must die to dwell in its habitation

How can one live with so many loves
Vulnerable to its beckoning call
It's almost better to not have loved but lived,
Than to be held captive to loves warring in the soul

IV.

Hear my cry oh love
For I am destitute of your graces
My thirsting soul seeks your pleasure,
Desiring the sweet touch of your lips
Like a madman confined to the prison of his fears
I search for ways to liberate my soul
Hoping to find the door that will set me free!

I feel as if my soul wants to run upon the heavens
Escaping this prison, void of the embrace of love
Love that accentuates a heightened desire
To be in your presence,
To lay upon your breast
To take refuge in your bosom
To lay naked before your eyes
Like the days before we desired to be like God!

Now we hide shamelessly behind
The pretense of understanding who we are.
We fall victim to the knowledge of a deceitful lust
As if falling upon a blade covered in blood
Lying in wait, drawn away of their own lusts, hungry to feed.

You pierce my soul!

Having received from the sweet breath of your lips,
I fight day and night in efforts to receive life, which stems from
You, oh love!
Having given of my precious fruit,
The fruit of my heart
The fruit of my mind
The fruit of my soul
The fruit of my being
I desire fruit in return but find unplanted seeds
Trapped in this prison of fears

Becoming numb to the vises keeping me bound
Substitutes, attempting to teach me lessons of love

I cry from the depths of my soul;
Clothed yet, naked
Feeling as if every eye can see the fallibility of my heart
While looking upon my soul, life gushing our profusely
Punctured by a blade, covered with fresh blood

Lust has a name with many faces
Love is a spirit for every man
When in search for love in different places
We're open to lusts deceitful hand

V.

Having gone through great extremes
Making ready for Love's arrival
Love's visitation has left me
In a state of bewilderment;
As if spring cleaning
Anticipating the dawning of new life
The joys of birds singing, and
The whistling of the trees played like a flute

Such season's change the countenance,
Causing us to open, empty out

Will the wind blow through my house?
With new Revelation of Love's desire, filling with such life
That as I journey through different seasons
Learn to draw from Love's truth
Resting in hope, knowing that Love
Must return

Instead of filling my soul
With the same empty smile, different faces
The same empty beauty, different vice
The same empty words, different manipulation
Hoping to pass the time
Hoping to escape the loneliness
Hoping to find a vessel
Not only to pour into, but
Pouring into me lessons of Love
Will we remain confined to a cell that has set limits to expression?

We choke the life out of love
Causing it to respond like puppets to strings
We limit love's movement, failing to embrace
Damaged by past woe,
Void of experience that pours from the heart and soul,
We remain mute to the sound and call of love.

When drawn to our intimate core, we retreat
Fearful of the darkness we may uncover,
Never expecting the Light of Love to shine through,
Never expecting illumination in such a way
That we fight every waking moment, desiring
Love's embrace
Not just in the arms of our love
Not merely enjoying loves, we share
But defeating the fear that has us confined to superficial kisses
Neglecting, the precious nectar from the fruit of our souls

There is no wonder why God desires love from our hearts
The city of our soul
Our flesh only satisfied by what it feels,
When praised or comforted will respond in gratification
Skillfully wielding its desire!

VI

How many books can we write about love?
How many words can communicate its depth?
How many flowers can express its intent?
How many chocolates accentuate its sweetness?

Is it love that we seek?
Do we consider the journey we beseech?
For Love is found where brokenness lay,
Love, found in more night than day
Love a road full of stones, thorns
Traveled by those seeking its glory, fueled by its fire

Are we sure?
Are we convinced?
Are we fully persuaded?
That, Love is what we are in search for?

How can our bowels of compassion stand by
Passing the stranger, wounded by the wayside?
We attend our services, praising God with blinded eyes,
We live our lives serving ME!
We laugh and smile with people we know
Quickly turning from those we might not know.
The sparkle in their eye might not be as bright,
Nor, the passion inside seem to fight,
Therefore, we meticulously pick our friends
Moreover, we dare not spend time on the outer ends of town
Where homeless are found
Where women of night roam around
Where poverty-stricken are bound- sleeping on the ground.

No, you dare not find me
Resurrecting homes on corners of different streets
Selling my soul for a bit to eat
But they love me, that's why they pay for me

Has anyone really loved me?
Do we take the time to search what has clouded, devoted love?
Oh, how we love to stay confined
To me, my friends,
My circle of influence
My color
My sister
My brother
When Love is calling for their sisters and brothers help.

Nevertheless, love has been so good to me
Therefore, I could never be
What I see, passing by!

VII

Listening to the rainfall; such serenity
Seems to quiet the war raging in the streets.
So much restless aggravations,
Hopelessness and fear,
Who wouldn't pray to God for peace?
You can hear it behind the smiles, and
See it just beyond the eye,
One must pay attention to subtle fluttering of the soul!

Sometimes our strength seems to escape our grasp,
Life seems to lie like the bones of our ancestors,
Transitioned to eternal rest or despair
Love seems to have suffocated
Drowned by dregs of sorrow.

Who can will life to be when life seems to will against us?

I can see the Almighty looking down with tears falling from his eyes
Hoping to cleanse the filth and stench of darkness from his creations heart
and mind
Wanting nothing more than to abide with his beloved
His beloved embracing Him!

I see the Almighty wondering why we have filled our earthen vessels with
every desire except Love, he has freely given
That none should perish
Yet, no one is willing to reach out his or her hand
In efforts to save their own flesh from dying.

Will we ever come to the place our soul's commune
With our fellow man.
Will we ever come to the place
We forgive, cleansing ourselves
By the tears that fall from our Everlasting Father?
Will we ever gain a passionate desire to experience Love

A Love that has power to sustain, empower, and nourish
Instead of a lust that devours, consumes and is never satisfied?

Will we ever lay down our lives that we may
Pour into the lives of those destitute of Love
Confident that heavens fountain will fill our cups
That we may never want,
That we may never hurt,
That we may never cry;
Lest we cry because Love has past,
Lest we cry because Love has been rejected,
Lest we cry while giving our lives
As a ransom, that life will continue to live!

I see the Almighty waiting patiently, with
Longsuffering, for his prodigals to find their way;
To find their way back to L O V E!

LIBERATION

It is in such place we dare not speak
Beseeching us to open our hearts to Love's Liberation
In deep, dark, despair we cringe in fetal position
Shivering, hoping it all will pass

Blanket over our heads
Eyes clinched shut
Holding our breath
Hoping the dark shadow of death will reproof
Musing the thoughts running through our mind
Praying internally that God hears our cry

The initial step out is the greatest of all
Fearing that no one will receive us as we are
Fearing that God will turn away
Fearing that we will be left alone through all our days

Many have considered us damaged goods
Having smiled yet unable to appropriate the good
Having desire to show that we earnestly love
Finding that we bitterly P U S H away

Asking God for chance after chance
We in fear receive opportunity
We in fear close up and run back to depression
Desiring life to be no more
Such excruciating pain to bear

Many have pushed us away!
Debilitating guilt

How do we push past this mirage of life-less-ness
Drowning in utter deprivation
A dessert of broken hearts and dreams
So many times, we run with passion
We run after love and the feeling of affirmation
So many ties, we blindly embrace
Smiles with hearts aimed for our destruction

In part, we are to blame, not taking time to understand
Other times we are victims and overcoming seems out of our reach
Will there ever be love?
Will I ever love?
Will I ever be loved?

Such piercing thoughts, for what my heart desired turned to my hurt
Now, trusting my heart, my mind, becomes an endless struggle
Second guessing every turn

I hear Love knocking on the door of my heart
Patient, steady, confident, reassuring
I want to move, so I open one eye to see if death is lurking

II

G O D

How compassionate G O D can be
Directly touching the heart
Whether stony, broken, indifferent
His love has way of softening, mending, and fortifying

So pure, attractive, comforting
Though compels such reverence
Willingly I long to submit to His Authority
Power in control

His presence a sweet fragrance
Refreshing breeze of morning air
Like the smell of warm cinnamon buns
Fresh ground coffee beans
The aroma of mint

Breathtaking, I welcome His presence
How can we hold to such brokenness
When our creator suffers to take us in
My eyes now open to the Light of His Glory

Shamefully I bow my head
Ignorant to the ignorance that lies in me
Tears fall from my eyes
Realizing he was there all the time- waiting to set me free

Like fairy tales that come true
All the pieces, all the fears, all doubt
Erased with one touch of His hand
Gentle caresses of His Spirit speak to my heart

O, my soul doth long for thee
O, my soul doth wait
I empty out my all to thee
My soul shall utter your Praise

Like Rivers of water gushing from within
I lift my hands in utter glee
G O D loosed, the chains that had me bound
G O D's Love has set me free

III

Oh, the Love
Oh, the Joy
Oh, the Peace
Which floods my soul!

No more want
No more worry
No more fear
That has control

Nights I've cried
Times I've tried
Hurtful ties
I've kept within

No longer rests
I am so blest
God gave His breath
New Life within

IV

Sleepless nights seem long and cold
From pain and fear being left alone
But with one touch or with one Word
My darkness turns to day

I thought this pain would never end
I felt so lost, controlled by sin
But the love of Christ it rescued me
By his blood I am redeemed

The Joy I once had I found a new
The day I gave my all to you
Oh, the peace that floods my soul
The day that I gave you complete control

Control of my heart, control of my mind
Turned over the fears I had inside
You sent your love and rescued me
Lord, I give you the Praise for the rest of my days

Love
I found in you

Joy
I found in you

Peace
I found in you

I will give you the praise
For the rest of my days

Love
Joy
Peace
Is found

Love
Joy
Peace
In You

Jesus

Love
Joy
And
Peace
Is found in you!

WOUNDED

The tears cried were from deep within
Cutting like a knife
The pain and uncertainty of life
Preserved, or shall it pass away?
Having done all to protect, love pushed away
The madness that circles my brain
Beating in my head
Thoughts unclear, feelings unstable
No one around to vent my frustrations
No one to pick up the call
Crying out to God in utter desperation
Help me! Silence the frustration
Of not connecting to love
Is it life?

Is it death?
Am I over-reacting?

Visions from heaven speak louder than
Voices from earth through skilled professions
It's appointed once for man to die; but before time?
Faith will cause you to speak what the eyes do not see
Rather deep routed convictions the heart believes
Hoping and patiently waiting for manifestation
The process humbling
Many times, bringing one to a place of brokenness
Soul and Spirit
Depressed because life is so precious
Yet love seems to close itself in

Pain has a way of distorting our view
Sometimes the only thing we can do is
Hide ourselves in a cave and think only of our survival
Fighting furiously to push loved ones out

Feeling as if there is nowhere to turn
No light of day
Everything closing in
Sheer hopelessness
Doing all we know to stay alive
I'm reminded, the pain of love

Looking in on loved ones paralyzed
Unable to see anyone else but themselves
Forsaking the rope to their salvation
From love looking in

Grace allows us to see another day
That we may learn to bear a little more
That we may bridle the tongue that will bless
The tongue that will curse in a moments, notice
Frustration has way of consuming and taking over
Yet, experience says, "Hold on"
Hold on 'til the pain subsides
Hold on 'til the tears are dried
Hold on 'til love can understand
Hold on 'til love sees your hand
Hold on 'til the smoke dissipates, and the winds have ceased
Hold on 'til faith has hope to believe
Hold on 'til settled and ready for embrace
Hold on 'til you have the strength to pray

It's not easy, sometimes complicated
The mind searching for peace
When love is fighting
When love wants to reach out
When love is pushed away
When love is paralyzed

Love is the only thing that can overcome fears
Therefore, we must learn to cry out when in need of Him
Christ's overcoming presence has way of bringing soundness
Soundness to mass confusion, intimate hurt and emotions
Uncontrolled
Releasing comforting presence and Light
Destroying the evil heart hardened in unbelief
Hoping the best in spite of gross darkness

Heal the wounded spirit
Strengthen the weakened hands
Revive the poor in spirit
Provide the fortitude to stand
It's in your care we commit our beloved
It's in your name we call
We humble ourselves awaiting your touch
With power to heal us all

TRANSITIONS

Another day goes by
Building upon stagnate blocks
Empty words
With sharp tips
Not meant to hurt
Only to understand
Holding to
What has slipped away
What has never been
A whisper to the wind
Standing on sea side foundations
Sunken deep in earths shell
Shaken by cumulous waves
Set a drift
To a restless sea
Tossed and driven
No place to rest no place to sleep
Raindrops falling one by one
Like madness running from my head
To the bottom of my foot
Soaked with anguish
Perplexed in utmost despair
Only the chill of night
The cold black sky
The uncertainty of tomorrow
Stare me in my face
Facing the storms
And the demons
That has me racing
To find meaning
To such dismal life

As I know it
Asking me questions
I must address
I must adhere to
I must embrace
I must answer to
The swell of angry waves
Trying to destroy
My vessel
Caring precious gifts
To yonder land
Full of inspiration
Keys to future locks
Manifesting future plans
And destinies
Learning
From the storms that plague me
Taking me through swift transitions
God carries your heart
As if you carried,
Precious jewels
Placing it safe
From harms, way
Adoring his treasure
Leaving it?
No never hiding it
 In the secret corridors
Of Heavens temple
Constantly in Omniscient

How then
Can we
Question things created
For what or whom
Rather let's learn from
The given task
Maturing us for
The greater question
Life may ask
Blowing upon the course
Of our existence
Tempting us from soundness
Grounded in Truth
In the eye of the storm is the greatest peace
You must go through the storm

Transitions

Reflections!

I.

Hear the cries see the tears
Blood so shed throughout the years
Shackles the chains the manipulative games
Taking the breath from those that were pained
Robbed of identity crisis was strange
Precious minds left hopeless deranged
Skinned to the bone were knuckles that paved
Freedoms that many enjoy on today

To know my mother was to lose my father
Taken from the home to find him why bother
Cries of a mother from deep within were much harder
For the "Massa's" delight of the "coming of age daughter"
Don't pick the flowers' mass 'a
Don't pick them why bother
The only man I've known has been the thief and the robber
Robbed me of my person stole away my heart
Crushed the very dreams of making a new start
Stole away my love gave him to another
Robbed him of his pride what was a friend, husband, and father
They have sown seeds of discord, division and dissention
Lied, cheated, among others not to mention
Lord help! For this false hope of security
Who is the devil I dream of? Is this devil the color of me?
Oh, the fight to be free!
Was it an illusion that bound me?
Oh, how do I be, in the land of the free?
I was stripped, programmed to be
Defamed, degraded, this life has me jaded
I thank God I made it
But did I really make it
Searching for identity with strong propensity
To survive even if it means giving me

That my family could be
Everything God created them to be
Take a deep look at me
I was born of whips and chains
I was stripped of my name
People ran as if I had the bubonic plague
I thought only animals knew the rage
That was tormenting me
As I fought vicariously
To see through the eyes of God
Ashamed to be me
People bemoaned me
Still they disowned me
Yet I haven't learned to be
They have not accepted me free

II.

Take a look at me now the object of affection
Round hips, beautiful lips, once a curse now the world's obsession
Broad shoulders and big noses, nappy hair and GQ poses
Wanting to be like, act like, and sound like
A force through-out the ages that made a name upon the pages, of
His-Story
Of who we were shackled and chained
But when I turn on the T.V. I see a huge black parade
My presence was daunting, so they just filmed my legs
Tried to film my moves but they could not catch the groove
Was I running or prancing, dancing or laughing,
Shouting the VIC-TOR-Y though they tried to capture me
They could never see
Life beyond the color of time
The color that mesmerized and left clouded the mind
The natural essence of character the bless-ed
Enduring the pain but through love expressive

They could record my voice but turned away my heart
Made millions off of me while inside falling apart
Had to sit in back of busses, the final word in cusses
You would think I was a stray dog I was eating off their lunches
Licking my sores and enduring the punches
Still I am esteemed the epitome of over-coming crutches
The silent voice heard in the cold cells of prison, was
Keep living, keep living, Black Man keep on living
Kill'em with your giving, giving while your living
Living while your loving, loving while their bugging
Keep their shoulders shrugging, my sister's they be hugging
Hugging why they're wanting to duplicate that special something
That special something from Tar Babies to ever man's dream
It's a sticky situation on how they love to cling to me

Oh, how they love my nappy hair, now they stop and stare
Beholding natural beauty envying natural booty
Don't you know you can't do me?
I remember how you wanted to spew me, OUT
I came from kings and queens; I don't give up I believe
Fulfilling dreams of the King and on to greater things
Revolutionizing generations healing broken nations
Riding the wave of freedom for people of color
They watch me lead them
As the voice of freedom cries water fills the eye
Opening blinded eyes destroying evil ties
Bondage and pressure no man should ever give
That's how we've live
Enduring the obscuring of a nation and deep degradation
This is the emancipation proclamation to a new generation

III.

Take a look around "pimp's and ho's" what's really going down
What happened to the fight to be found
In community, building stronger family, unity between you and me
Without hope the people perish for they can't see, there way out
We've forgotten what it's all about
Devouring, malicious, hostile, belligerent

Push back the line, seek for the divine
Plan of Christ for your mind, look beyond human eyes

Our women shaking their rumps, hypnotized by the funk
Brother's selling their soul, just to sport some gold
Families falling apart cause mommy and daddy have no heart
We wonder why Bobby and Sue have no clue
Principle is a word of the past, now we glamorize all that's bad
The voice of rebellion is raising the roof from a generation with no couth
With freedom comes responsibility but now we see the inability
To nurture the heartbeat of humanity clouded by deplorable calamity
Lesbianism, adultery, debauchery, sorcery, homosexuality, it's killing me
Lewd improprieties
Freed,
Only to be enslaved by heart, mind, and soul
Tell me when did we lose control?
Let's look back to the day of old
When justice was worth fighting for
Now justice has become the whore
No one knows what is right or wrong anymore
We need to step up and settle the score.

Put the hedges back up, raise the respect back up
Fill the love back up, make the devil back up
Bring the peace back up, though evils act up
Bring the faith back up and hope back up
Lift Jesus back up, Hope in God back up
We need to stop acting up, pull our pants back up
Close our shirts back up, zip the zipper back up
Pull that belt back up, when our children act up
We'll make the devil back up, when our faith is stacked up

Through spiritual eyes we see eternities beginning
Manifested in the faith we are living
The love of Christ in our hear tis the beginning
Let's get to living, let's get to living, people of all color around the world
Let's get to living
In Jesus name!

Reflections

Young Black and Beauty-Full 2002

Seen as Generation X
Negative connotations
Cloud the minds
Of this young Beauty-Full nation
The weights of past lives
And pressures
Yoke the shoulders
Of our youth
In their endeavors
To reach higher ground
Higher learning
Ears burning
For knowledge
Wisdom
Corrupted in this
Political Social system
Which has them

Switch'n
Switch'n

How can you build on solid foundations
When grounded in sand
What happened to woman and man?
Man and woman
Neighborhoods
Communities
Working to raise
Children free
You put it on the church
That's one entity
The rest is up
To you and me

Whatch'a gonna do
When buck shots be gunn'n
Everyone is runn'n
For protection took discipline out the home
And gave it to the dogs
Whoop'ns never left me scarred
Still my life was hard
Train up a child in the way they should go
And they will get there
But who cares
Now that we are
Free?

Struggle draws a nation together
Once the struggle's gone
To each his own something's wrong
Wonder why we've got so many
Sad, sad, songs

Young, Black, and Beauty-Full
Our hands should be duty full
Putting prayer back in schools
Finding without God
Kids act a fool
Man that ain't cool
So much expression
In the life they're professing
Still we sit back
Sip our white wine
Don't want to listen
To the voice of the youth
Then wonder why
We are missing
Chances to bridge the gap
That has us all set back

For you can't press for tomorrow
When you have no tomorrow
To look forward to
What can we do?
It's up to me and you
If we put God first
The making is I the work
Shame if ya' feelings hurt
And hurting
And we be
Hurting
For we're all one blood
One nation
Under God
Indivisible
With liberty
What happened to, Justice for all

Young Black and Beauty-Full

...But Chains! 2002

It never stops
The soul ties
In Afro-American lives
Survival of the fittest
Enduring pains and cries
Divided in natural realm
Yet spiritual eyes
On the same plain
Still haven't bound the pain
Searching
For the means to gain
Momentum toward the vision
We've longed to obtain
The foundation was laid
Through sweat and blood
That paved the way
To brighter days
Looking through dark views
A dark past
Dark shadows
Which seem to speak louder than the living
Always giving and giving and giving
'Til the skin from our knuckles reach the bone
From the bone to the grave-yard
A life that's hard
Though freedom
Has left me unbarred

Looking back
To the whip lashes on my back
Sa-clash, sa-clash!
Liberation through knowledge
Sa-clash, sa-clash!
The right to vote saga
Sa-clash, sa-clash!
The dream of the preach 'a man
Sa-clash, sa-clash!
The revolutionary movement
Of the Black Panther man
Sa-clash, sa-clash!
Women's liberation
Sa-clash, sa-clash!
The colored's vindication
Sa-clash!
By any means necessary
Sa-clash, sa-clash, sa-clash!
All these lashes to my back
Down through time
While I'm removing the scales
That has you blind
The world as we know it
The politics
The schisms
That have me ill'n
When all they want to do
Is take the food
From my children
And your children
Then show me movies of killing
Black is bad
So black man equals villain
What world do you live in?

I'm born a man
I will die a man
My nature is to fight
With the work of my hands
With the voice that I speak
Points to the end
For the Spirit of God resides
Where no man
Wanted to go
No man wanted to see
Still,
I got nothing but love
No hate lives inside me
Graced with Spirit
That runs like steams
I flow eternally
My promise is heavenly things
Heavenly goals
What natural thing
Can hold
Me
Mold me
Shape me
Tried to rape me
But it's too late, see
I had a talk with God
Found out he made me
From the dust of the ground
I'm naturally brown
On my way down, I'll be found
In my natural home

My spirit
Back to where it belongs
In the arms of God
Forever to reign
I must endure the pain
Endure the pain, brotha's
Endure the pain, sista's
Endure the pain
For we
Ain't
Got
Nothing to lose

But Chains!

Fly Caged Bird Fly 2001

Fly Caged Bird Fly
Fly to unseen dimensions
Fly to new heights above the lethargic prison of your mind.
Above the "aint-gonna-be's" and discrepancies,
That causes you to rewrite the pages of your authenticities.
Above the shoot me downs and hand me downs
To this family and that family,
This school and that school,
This world and that world,
Fly to the edge of the universe.
Explore galaxies and suns that leave you questioning,
Is something else out there?
Far above the storms that bring perilous times to earth's inhabitants,
The circle of drama that leaves us hoping for a better life to live
Stretch your wings and soar
Like the eagles dancing across their playground
Going higher and higher and higher
Confident that their integrity keeps them safe from the curve
Llife can throw
Form the hunter's gun that keeps them bound
Close to the ground
Spread your wings Caged Bird and soar
Fly to the horizon that captivates your mind every morning
Far from the winters that plague your soul
Far from the doubts trapping you behind closed doors
Far from the hurts that press, you sore
Fly 'til you can't fly no more
Spread your wings Caged Bird and fly

Strengthen the stroke of your passion with each flap of your wing
Sing the songs of freedom that morning birds sing
Circle in observation ponder the next move to make
Then swoop for the kill as opportunity waits
Sit with a Bold chest, Peace and Dignity
Knowing the best is yet to come
The prize of your destiny
Fly to the utmost for no reason at all
For God made you to soar he didn't make you to fall
Soar to the end of promise breaking barriers of fear
Soar to the twilight at the end of your night
Soar Caged Bird Soar
'Til the words run off the pages
Through His-story, Her-story in your flight throughout the ages
Spread your wings and fly again
For your Mother, Father, Grandma, Grandpa, Aunts, Uncles,
Cousins, Niggas, who paved the way
Opening the prison doors that would try to bind you one day
Fly through the Dream of the Prophets and Wise Men
That manifest itself with time
It's time to flap your wings and fly!
Fly Caged Bird fly
Away
From the prison that binds

Freedom! Fly!

TSU NA MI

Every morning I wake
I thank the Lord
For another dawning
He didn't have to let me live,
But he did
Granting me the chance to speak life
To those sleep walking
Sleep talking
Programmed like robots
Stalking
For the next hustle
The next crime
The next clouded mind
Eyes filled with blood
Like the color of red wine
Don't you know the blind can't lead the blind?
They both fall into ditches
Now we have an epidemic
Stepping on your brother's back to get riches
Shiftless
Present day living
Is not measured by the things you have obtained
For they could be washed away by the rain

TSU NA MI

Present day economy
One day you have it
Then you don't
Families choke
By the mere fact,
They were sitting on top of the world
Now they find themselves on street corners, dark alleys
Rock bottom floors flat on their backs
Their dreams taken
Like waking to the morning sun
Dreams now a thought
A mere agitation of what is to come
See
Hour house is not a home
With couches and chairs
Tables and pairs of shoes
You don't wear anyway
Just self-indulgence of how
You've got it this way
Home
Is where the heart will roam
To find security, comfort, peace
To be the essence of me
Yet, losing all I am when losing all my bling, bling things
Trying to pick up the pieces, but
Can't put the pieces back together
That's p u z z l I n g!

TSU NA MI

No one warned me
No one told me
That what I possess
Is not the essence of me
Trying to find the image of me
Through pants hanging down
Below my knees
Degrading me
Don't' you know a family was cursed
From looking at the nakedness of me
 A
Lot
Like
What this nation is destined to be~ yet I
Walk with my swagger
Watch as my princesses and queens stagger
As I reach over try and grab her, them
Then wonder why the whole world laughs at her
No trick, no treat
Many enslaved by systematic slavery, thus
The cloud of darkness
Hovering around me
That's how they color me
Has my life been minimized
To drinking forty's and getting high
Trapping dimes
And slapping five
Make sure you get it on the black-hand-side

We speak of pride
We've given ourselves the black eye!
A whole nation
Now gyrates to our black vindication
Feeling cause we talk'n loud
We've gained a sense of equalization
Rather
A voice yelling in the wind
Turning in the wind
Moving with the wind
Heard a mere second
Then gone with the wind
Like a mist that evaporates
For it has no weight to fall
So, I am here to drop the bomb

B O O M!

TSU NA MI

Rushing in like a current
Can't be contained
Destroying superficial ideologies
God's creation deranged
It's not about the money, power, fortune, or fame
Somebody tell my sista's, stop
Swinging hips in lustful serenades
Pimped so long
Now embracing the game
Forsaking the shame
Ma dilly, dilly, dilly, D
Man
They have their own game
Trapp'n nigga's to take their name
Snatching babies to make their pockets phat
A foolish masquerade
Everybody ain't dead beat daddy sperm donors
Whipped by devilish masquerades
From a 36' 24' 36' dame
Working the judicial system just to be paid
Swinging their hips
Turning their tricks
Flaunting their whips
Stacking their chips
Loading their clips
Shaking their?
Licking their lips
Waiting for their next hit
Skin-tight!

Ever wonder why ya' daughters don't turn out right
Mother ya' wrong and don't want to get right
Sweet mother from earth
Losing their worth
The devil gave birth
To a wicked work
Swinging to a different tune
Running directly to their doom
Won't let go the clutches of sin
Even when face firing and brimstone
Remember
Lot's
Wife!

TSU NA MI

How could I ever reach
The purpose of God
If I never understand
I'm created to be
The essence of a king
The holiness of a priest
The prophetic voice of a prophet
Speaking to situations
Commanding it to stop
Commanding it to live
We all have a story to give
That others may survive their plight
Together we can work it for the good
So many are dancing in the night
Enjoying the season of sin
Hoping darkness never ends
When seeing the light, they cringe
Finding excuse of not to live
Of not becoming a son
We'd rather run
100 miles and running
Someone said
If you're scared go to church
But they are running
Searching for connection
Purpose to their affection
Empty in their profession
Unanswered aggression
Taking careless chances
Unprotected romances
Lead you down a road
In pursuit of happiness and stories untold

When will we stand, break the mold?
When will we stop selling our souls for gold?
When will we stop chasing dreams to be seen?
When will we stop defiling our queens?
When will we stop accepting filth for precious things?
When will we take our seats as kings?
For the wide road leads to a party in hell
Where all the gansta's yell
Where all the wicked dwell
Where all the ignorant fell
Wake up!
Don't get caught in the night
Look up, can you see the light?
Christ can fix every wrong, lead you right
Down the path of righteousness where His glory shines bright
Stand up and fight
Stand up and fight
Stand up and fight
The fight of faith
Before it's too late
Before
It's
Too
Late

TSU NA MI

83

Young, Black and Beauty-Full 2009

Young, Black and Beauty-Full we remain
Such overcoming spirit birthed through pain
The Christ who died paving the way
Through lives of those who perished through trade
Resting on bottoms of sea floors
Whispers of grandeur washed up upon seas shores
Compels one to press through, vision to see more
Than me, my family, my four, and no more
Such pressure has birthed precious living jewels
Through those fulfilling the Golden Rule
Stretched beyond comprehension
That's why I can't help but see
The color of you
The color of me
So Beauty-Full
So lively
So Exciting
So, inviting
Tell me your story
Help me understand the glory
That radiates upon your face
Tell me how you destroyed color lines
That kept a nation color confined
Through your prophetic dreams
Through your songs of black and white
The brave the bold the beautiful
Lead the fight
Sacrificing lives on front lines
Down through time
The Preacher
Educator
Emancipator
The Innovator
The world will take note

That truth will endure
Then eyes will see
Love in the heart of humanity
Is God in you, is God in me
A force that cannot be stopped by slavery
Race-ism, any-ism
White sheets
Dogs or violence in the streets
Rape or murder while we sleep
Cannot stop the heart beat
Cannot deter victory we speak
Cannot prevent destiny to be
What God has declared
Shall come to pass
Will we search for The Path
That we may rest in heaven's blessedness?
I must profess
What I believe
That Christ is the Savior who wants all to believe
That God has colored us all with such Beauty
Want Chocolate
Caramel
Coffee
Vanilla Cream
Want Coco Brown
Take your pick
What's your liking
So many striking
Images
Of you and me
The Beauty of it all
Makes me happy to be
Young
Black
And
Beauty-Full

Black Soul

Black Soul
Use to move and groove you
Say It Loud
I'm Black and I'm proud
With Yo' Bad Self
Evoked a voice
Liberating the oppressed
Caused you to hold your head up high
Though guns went off in the sky
Though fires were set ablaze
While blood shot tears filled the eyes
Yet the rhythm, would stir the soul
So deep
One could not help but speak
Seeking higher plane
Liberation
Vindication
Elation
Beating in the S O U L
Music
Music that gave a voice
Black Rich Music
Beating to the heart of the matter
Louder than shot-gun scatter
Prophetic of coming matter
Revealing current dilemma
Exposing hidden agenda
Did you read the writing on the wall?
It's very superstitious
How dominoes fall
In succession
You can feel the aggression
Through Soul Expression

Black Soul

Always possessed black gold
So many professed and tried to mold
Invisible life you cannot hold
A voice that flowed from the soul

What happened to Black Soul?
That makes me shame to hold, *UP*
The voice now expressed
In such ***Black Soul***

Though dark and deep
Yet a light would speak
Pushing you to reach
For dark dreams
In the distance
Perseverance with vigorous persistence
Until the sweat dropped
And the beat popped
In your soul like a drum
Victorious drum
Stand up and fight drum
Drop it on the one drum

Can still move me
Can still use me

To promote a life of hope
Before the Lord spews us, out
Lukewarm
Washed up and no good
O how we love to live hood
Signifying and no good

Black Soul

Now corrupted black gold
All about booties you hold
Unashamed to keep it on the down low
How we love Black Soul

Somebody help me destroy the mold
Our youth are selling their soul for gold
It's time to wake up
It's time to wake up

Black Soul

As we press to reach for tomorrow
Let's not forget about today
Cherish the laughter, joy, and sorrow
Lest precious moments slip away

Black Soul

Was more than music to snap fingers
Was Spirit-filled message that yet lingers
In subconscious mind
It helped refine
A nation created to endure the times

Black Soul

Never meant to be a drug house
To get your fix the music route
Rather a light of hope
To help cope
Through this life to set us free
Not freedom that abuses
Violating the human spirit
Destroying the image of the Divine

But promotes peace
Fortifies nations, a people, the hopeless
Bringing life to the streets

Black Soul

The gun shot in the face of oppression
The high from the heaviness of deep depression
The clarity in midst of clouded professions
The birthing of a nation through rhythmic impressions

Black Soul

Cannot go back from whence it came
Must seek the Lord to find its name
Must stop degradation from the CD spin
And let the Light come in
Enter in

B L A C K S O U L

CPSIA information can be obtained
at www.ICGtesting.com
Printed in the USA
LVHW071728210821
695820LV00001B/6